Acting Rhymes

A. & C. BLACK LTD. LONDON

In this same series
Counting Rhymes
Rhythm Rhymes
Speech Rhymes
Nonsense Rhymes

Also by Clive Sansom
Speech and Communication in the Primary School

Second edition 1975 Reprinted 1976, 1977, 1980
© 1975 A. & C. Black Ltd 35 Bedford Row London WC1R 4JH
ISBN 0 7136 1541 9
Printed in Great Britain by Tindal Press

CONTENTS

INTRODUCTION

All the rhymes in this book can be acted, mimed, or played as games with a group. The characters within the rhymes are many and varied, calling for a corresponding variety of interpretation; the lively rhythms and expressive use of words encourage spontaneity and individuality.

The rhymes are suitable for children of from 5 to 12. They are arranged in three sections according to age suitability, starting with verses for the youngest children. At the end of the book is a special note for teachers and suggestions for using the rhymes.

Giant

The tall, stern Giant moves
With long, strong, even strides.
(Every little boy who sees him
Runs away and hides.)

The Giant, angry, grumpy, surly,
Marches over house and hill.
(Every little boy is hiding
Very quiet and still.)

On the Giant trudges glumly;
Gruff and grim he takes his way.
(All the little boys are happy—
Out they come to play!)

Clive Sansom

Callers

The Man-in-the-Van sells ices,
    Ting-a-ling; ting, ting-a-ling!
The Man-in-the-Van sells ices,
    One, two and three.

The Milkman leaves us bottles,
    Milk-O; milk-O!
The Milkman leaves us bottles,
    One, two and three.

The Postman brings our letters,
    Rat-tat; rat-tat-tat!
The Postman brings our letters,
    One, two and three.

What other people call?

Boy and Owl

A little boy went into a barn
    And lay down on some hay.
An owl came out, and flew about,
    And the little boy ran away.

Rabbit Rhymes

1

See the bunny sleeping
All the afternoon.
Let us come and wake him
With a merry, merry tune.

Oh, how still . . .
Is he ill? . . .
WAKE UP NOW!

Australian song-game

2

Bunny rabbit, bunny rabbit,
　　Hop, hop, hop;
Bunny rabbit, bunny rabbit,
　　Stop, stop, stop.
I've raced you, I've chased you,
　　Far and wide:
Bunny rabbit, bunny rabbit,
　　Run away and hide!

Evelyn Abraham

Catch-Rhymes

Can you keep in step to these?

1

Hippety-hop
To the barber's shop
To buy three sticks of candy.
One is for you,
And one for me,
And one for my sister Mandy.

American rhyme

2

Dancing Dolly had no sense,
She bought a fiddle for eighteen pence,
And the only tune that she could play
Was "Sally, get out of the donkey's way!"

London street-game

3

Fiddle me up to London Town,
And fiddle me down to Dover.
I'll dance as long as the music plays,
But I'll stop when the playing is over.

Hilda Adams

4

One, two, three,
You can't catch me.
Here I go, there I go,
One, two, three.   *(Repeat)*

Evelyn Abraham

5

Here we come galloping, galloping,
     galloping,
Galloping over the down.
Robin is riding a dapple-grey pony,
My little pony is brown.

Hilda Adams

Miss Periwinkle

Said little Periwinkle,
Both her eyes a-twinkle:
"I'm going to the Ball tonight."
But nobody could wake her,
Hard as they might shake her,
Her eyes were shut so tight!

Geese

"Chick chick chatterman,
How much are your geese?"
—"Chick chick chatterman,
Two cents apiece."
—"Chick chick chatterman,
That's too dear."
—"Chick chick chatterman,
Chase you out of here!"

American game

Ten Little Mice

Ten little mice sat down to spin.
Kitty came by and popped her head in.

"What are you doing, my ten little men?"
—"We're weaving coats for gentlemen."

"Shall I come in and cut off your threads?"
—"Oh no, Mrs Kitty, you'll bite off our
    heads!"

Gardening

"Last weekend in the garden,
What did you find to do?"
[—"I pushed the lawn-mower."]
(Demonstrates)
—"Did you? Did you?
No wonder the garden grew!"

Now go on

Who's That Ringing?

"Who's that ringing
    at the front door bell?"
  "Miaou, miaou, miaou:
I'm a little black cat
    and I'm not very well,
  Miaou, miaou, miaou!"
"Then put your nose
    in this dish of mutton fat,
  (Miaou, miaou, miaou!)
For that's the way
    to cure a little cat."
  "Miaou, miaou, miaou!"

Early in the Morning

A little boy got out of bed—
It was only six o'clock—
And through the window popped
    his head
And spied a crowing cock.

The little boy said, "Mr Bird,
Pray tell me, who are you?"
This was the answer that he got:
"Cock-a-doodle-doo!"

Author unknown

Rhymes about Robin

I

Little Robin Redbreast
Sat upon a tree.
Up went tabby-cat,
Down went he.

Down came tabby-cat,
Away Robin ran.
"I'm little Robin Redbreast:
Catch me if you can!"

Little Robin Redbreast
Came to visit me.
This is what he whistled:
"Thank you for my tea!"

3

Little Jenny Wren
    Fell sick upon a time;
In came Robin Redbreast
    And brought her cake and wine.

"Eat well of my cake, Jenny,
    Drink well of my wine."
—"Thank you, Robin, kindly:
    You shall be mine."

Jenny she got well
    And stood upon her feet,
And told Robin plainly,
    "I love you not a bit."

Robin, very angry,
    Hopped upon a twig:
"Out upon you, fie upon you,
    Bold-faced jig!"

What are you going to be?

What are you going to be?
What are you going to be?
I shall be a Lady—
That's the life for me! . . .

What are you going to be?
What are you going to be?
I shall be a Soldier—
That's the life for me! . . .

Paul Edmonds

Riding on an Engine

Here we go to London,
Riding on an engine.
See the little chuff-chuffs
Standing in a row.
The man upon the engine
Pulls his little lever—

TCH! TCH!
OOF! OOF!
Off we go!

Author unknown

Tales of Two Frogs

I

A little green frog in a pond am I,
Hoppity, hoppity, hop.
I sit on a little leaf, high and dry,
And watch all the fishes as they swim by—
Splash!—how I make the water fly!
Hoppity, hoppity, hop.

Author unknown

2

Mr Frog jumped out of the pond one day
And found himself in the rain.
"Oh dear, I'll get wet and I may catch
cold!"
So he jumped in the pond again.

Traditional

Whirling Leaves

Like a leaf or feather
In the windy, windy weather,
We whirl around,
And twirl around,
And all fall down together.

Author unknown

The Clever Rabbit

There was a little Rabbit
    who was lying in his burrow . . .
When the Dingo[1] rang him up to say
    he'd call on him tomorrow.

But the Rabbit thought it better
    that the Dingo did not meet him;
So he found another burrow
    and the Dingo didn't eat him.

[1] wild dog

D. H. Souter

Candles

"Bring me a hundred candles,"
The lovely lady said,
"That I may have a hundred flames
To light me up to bed."

They brought a hundred candles
And made the dark stairs bright.
"I thank you," said the lady,
"Good night, good night, good night."

Ruth Ainsworth

The Mice and the Cat

One mouse, two mice,
Three mice, four,
Stealing from their tunnel,
Creeping through the door.

Softly! softly!
Don't make a sound—
Don't let your little feet
Patter on the ground.

There on the hearth-rug,
Sleek and fat,
Soundly sleeping
Lies old Tom Cat.

If he should hear you,
There'd be no more
Of one mouse, two mice,
Three mice, four.

So please be careful
How far you roam.
If you wake him
He'll chase you all HOME!

Clive Sansom

Miss Muffet and Friend

1

Little Miss Muffet
Sat on a tuffet,
Eating her curds and whey.
There came a big spider
Who sat down beside her
And frightened Miss Muffet away.

Traditional

2

Little Miss Muffet
Sat on a tuffet,
Eating her Irish stew.
Along came a spider
And sat down beside her—
So she ate *him* up, too!

Author unknown

3

Little Miss Tuckett
Sat on a bucket,
Eating some peaches and cream.
There came a grasshopper
And tried hard to stop her,
But she said, "Go away, or I'll scream!"

Author unknown

Meeting in the Street

"Good morning, Mrs Grant Mackay;
I often see you passing by.
That's a pretty child with you.
Such a little lady, too!"

"Thank you, Mrs McIntyre;
It's *your* child we most admire.
Most politely, two by two,
May we take a walk with you?"

"Delighted, Mrs Grant Mackay!
We never have—I can't think why.
The sun is bright, such lovely weather:
Let us walk the park together."

Canadian rhyme

We're All Nodding

We're all nodding; nid, nod, nodding,
We're all nodding in our house at home.
With a turning in, and a turning out,
This way, that way, turning round about,
We're all nodding; nid, nod, nodding,
We're all nodding in our house at home.

Fruit Market

"What is in your basket?
    What have you to sell?"
—"Pawpaws, plums and pineapples;
    Oranges as well."

"May I take some passion-fruit?"
    —"If you have the money:
Also pots of melon jam
    And frangipani honey."

Clive Sansom

My Pigeon-House

My pigeon-house I open wide
    and set my pigeons free.
They fly about on every side,
    then perch on the nearest tree.

But when they return
    from their merry, merry flight,
I close my doors
    and say good night.
Coo, coo, coo-oo.
Coo, coo, coo-oo.

Author unknown

Follow-My-Leader

Follow him up
   and follow him down,
Follow him round
   and about the town.

   Where he will take you to
      nobody knows,
   But follow your leader
      wherever he goes.

Follow him here,
   follow him there,
Follow on after him
   everywhere.

   Where he will take you to
      nobody knows,
   But follow your leader
      wherever he goes.

H. S. Bennett

Tadpoles

Ten little tadpoles
    playing in a pool.
"Come," said the water-rat,
    "come along to school.
Come and say your tables,
    sitting in a row."
And all the little tadpoles said,
    "No, no, no!"

Ten little tadpoles
    swimming in and out,
Racing and diving
    and turning round about.
"Come," said their mother,
    "dinner-time, I guess."
And all the little tadpoles cried,
    "Yes, yes, yes!"

Rose Fyleman

Old Green Gnome

The old green gnome,
He hobbles, hobbles, hobbles,
With his sack on his back
He wobbles, wobbles, wobbles
To his funny little shop
Where he cobbles, cobbles, cobbles
All the shoes for fairy folk
For dancing on the Green.

Maisie Cobby

The King of Candy

The King of Candy lost his crown,
His courtiers saw his Royal Frown.
They hunted high, they hunted low.
"Where can it be?"—"None of us know."

They hunted left, they hunted right,
They found it in the Isle of Wight.
They took it to the King, who cried:
"I know it's mine: my name's inside!"

He was so pleased, he made a speech,
And handed a threepenny-bit to each.

Anne Harding Thompson

Coming to School

Coming to school,
Coming to school,
I saw a Postman
Coming to school . . .

Coming to school,
Coming to school,
I saw a Policeman
Coming to school . . .

Who came next?

Old Dame

Where have you been?
To the wood.
What for?
To pick up sticks.
What for?
To light my fire.
What for?
To boil my kettle.
What for?
To cook some of your chickens!

Old country game

The Tired Caterpillar

A tired old caterpillar went to sleep
In a hole in the forest, snug and deep.
And he said, as he softly curled
   in his nest . . .
"Crawling is pleasant, but rest is best."

He slept through the winter long and cold,
All tightly up in his blanket rolled,
But at last he woke on a warm Spring day
To find that Winter had gone away.

He felt and fluttered his golden wings:
No need to crawl over sticks and things.
"Oh, earth is good for a butterfly,
But the sky is best when we learn to fly!"

American rhyme

The Sheep and the Wolf

Sheep, sheep, come home!
   We are afraid.
What are you afraid of?
   The Wolf.
The Wolf's not here—
He's not been near
For many a year,
So sheep, sheep, come home!

Old country game

The Little Hunter

There was once a little boy
Who had a little horse,
And he said, "I'll shoot a rabbit,
A rabbit in the gorse,
   With a bing, bang, bong,
   And a ding, dang, dong."

He hunted in the gorse
And he climbed a little hill,
And he fired his little gun
With a right good will—
   With a bing, bang, bong,
   And a ding, dang, dong.

The gun made such a noise
That he tumbled off his horse,
And there he sat and cried
Among the prickly gorse,
   With a bing, bang, bong,
   And a ding, dang, dong.

Then up came Granny Green
And took the hunter home
And gave him currant cake
And honey from the comb,
   With a bing, bang, bong,
   And a ding, dang, dong.

*Translated from the French
by Rose Fyleman*

Willie Wilkie

Wee Willie Wilkie
      runs through the town,
Upstairs and downstairs
      in his night-gown,
Tapping at the window,
      crying at the lock:
"Are the children in their beds?
      It's past eight o'clock!"

The Very Tiny Man

We met a very tiny man,
   A pixie or an elf.
The ear of corn he carried
   Was as tall as himself.

He bore it on his shoulder—
   It was bristly and round.
We watched him stepping past us,
   And we didn't make a sound.

We didn't make a sound at all,
   But he sharply turned his head
And dropped his burden on the ground:
   "I thought you were in bed.

"You're very late about tonight.
   I hate to make a fuss,
But from ten o'clock till six o'clock
   This field belongs to Us.

"But you may stay this once, I think,
   You may walk upon the grass;
Only don't step on the buttercups
   And daisies as you pass.

"You may stay this very once, perhaps,
    You may stay, perhaps, and look;
Only don't pick any mushrooms
    That grow by the brook."

He turned his head away from us,
    He hoisted up his pack;
He strutted briskly down the path
    And never once looked back.

Clive Sansom

No Pleasing Them

Two ducks went waddling down the lane.
Said one to the other, "What beautiful
    rain!"

Two children ran to the door with a
    frown.
"We can't go out while the rain pours
    down!"

The Clerk of the Weather scratched
    his head:
"You can't please *every*one," he said.

Author unknown

Hoppity

Christopher Robin goes
Hoppity, hoppity,
Hoppity, hoppity, hop.
Whenever I tell him
Politely to stop it, he
Says he can't possibly stop.

If he stopped hopping, he couldn't go
    anywhere;
Poor little Christopher
Couldn't go anywhere . . .
That's why he *always* goes
Hoppity, hoppity,
Hoppity,
Hoppity,
Hop.

A. A. Milne

The Canny Mouse

There was a wee-bit[1] mousikie,
  That lived in Gilberaty-O.
It couldna' get a bit o' cheese
  For cheatie-pussie-cattie-O.
Said mousie tae the cheesikie,
  "O fain wad I be at ye O,
If it werena' for the cruel paws
  O' cheatie-pussie-cattie-O."

Scottish rhyme

[1] tiny

The Hungry Hunter

There was a hungry hunter
Went hunting for a hare,
But where he hoped the hare would be
He found a hairy bear!

"I'm very, very hungry:
I *get* hungry now and then."—
The hunter turned head-over-heels
And hurried home again.

Author unknown

Here Comes a Knight

Here comes a Knight a-riding,
   To the Castle he has come;
The Lady Anne puts out her head:
   "My lord is not at home.—

"There's no-one but the children,
   And chickens in the pen."
The Knight upon his charger,
   He says to Lady Anne:

"And are the children naughty
   Or are the children good?"
"Oh, very bad indeed," says she,
   "They won't do as they should."

Says he: "Then I'll not have them,
   No use are they to me."
He turns him to the rightabout
   And home again rides he.

Translated from the German
by Rose Fyleman

Raggle Taggle Rabbit-Skins

Raggle Taggle Rabbit-Skins,
 you sly old Fox,
You can't keep rabbits
 in a cardboard box!
We'll nibble and we'll gnaw,
 and we'll bite and we'll chew,
We'll wriggle and we'll push
 and we'll hop right through.
Raggle Taggle Rabbit-Skins,
 you sly old Fox,
You'll NEVER keep rabbits
 in a cardboard box!

Raggle Taggle Rabbit-Skins,
 the sly old Fox,
Shut up all his rabbits
 in a cardboard box.
The rabbits they scrabbled,
 the rabbits they scraped,
They made a huge hole
 and each rabbit escaped.
Raggle Taggle Rabbit-Skins,
 you sly old Fox,
You've lost every rabbit
 in the cardboard box!

Mollie Clarke

Little Cock-Sparrow

A little cock-sparrow sat on a tree,
And he chirruped, he chirruped,
    so merry was he—

Till a boy came along with his bow
    and his arrow,
Determined to shoot at that little
    cock-sparrow.

"This little cock-sparrow will make
    a good stew,
And his giblets will make me a pasty
    too."

—"Oh no, little huntsman, I *won't*
    make a stew!"
So he flapped his wings, and away
    he flew.

The Rabbit and the Fox

A rabbit came hopping, hopping,
Hopping along in the park.
"I've just been shopping, shopping,
I must be home before dark."

A fox came stalking, stalking,
Stalking from under a tree.
"Where are you walking, walking?
Why don't you walk with me?"

The rabbit went hopping, hopping,
Hopping away from the tree.
"I've just been shopping, shopping,
I *must* be home for my tea."

"Come with me, bunny, bunny—
Bunny, you come with me;
I'll give you some honey, honey,
I'll give you some honey for tea."

"I can't be stopping, stopping,
I'm far too busy today"—
And the rabbit went hopping, hopping,
Hopping away and away.

Clive Sansom

Hector Protector

Hector Protector was dressed all in green
Hector Protector was sent to the Queen.
The Queen did not like him—no more did
    the King,
So Hector Protector was sent home again

Robin and Richard

Robin and Richard
Were two pretty men;
They lay in bed
Till the clock struck ten.

Then up starts Robin,
And looks at the sky:
"Oh, brother Richard,
The sun's very high.

"You go before
With bottle and bag,
And I will come after
On little Jack Nag."

The Witch and the Wizard

Those taking part :

Tree	Bricks and Stones
Witch	Wizard
Boy	Girl

At the back of the stage or acting-space is a large Tree, made by two groups of children. To the left of this are two piles of Bricks and Stones, also children.

Tree :   Green leaves are swaying
                Like waves of the sea.
Upper Tree : We are the branches,
Lower Tree : And we are the tree.

Tree :   Cool, shady branches;
                Strong, sturdy tree.
Lower Tree : Leaves at the top—tell us,
                What can you see?

Upper Tree : We see bricks on the hillside
                And stones in the ditch,
                A little girl running—
                And here comes a Witch!

Witch comes in, from the left, dragging a Girl.

Witch :	Grey stones in the ditch,
	Red bricks on the ground,
	Build me a castle
	As round as round.

Stones and Bricks rise, and form a circle.
The Witch pushes the girl inside, crying.

A good place for crying,
A long time for tears.
You shall stay in this castle
A thousand years!

Witch goes off left. Boy comes in from right.

Boy :	Little girl, little girl,
	Why won't you play?
Girl :	A wicked old Witch
	Has shut me away.

Boy :	Don't cry, little girl,
	But listen to me.
	I know a kind Wizard
	Who'll set you free.

Boy goes off right.

Tree :	Green leaves are swaying
	Like waves of the sea.
Upper Tree :	We are the branches,
Lower Tree :	And we are the tree.

Tree :   Cool, shady branches;
                Strong, sturdy tree.
Lower Tree : Leaves at the top—tell us,
                What can you see?

Upper Tree : We see a large castle
                That's round and tall—
                A boy running back,
                And a Wizard and all!

*Boy comes in from right again, with
Wizard.*

Wizard :   Grey stones from the country,
                Red bricks from the town—
                Abra-cadabra!
                All fall down!

*Bricks and Stones collapse where they
were standing.   Witch comes in, from
left, in a great temper.*

Witch :   Oh, you horrid old Wizard!
                        (Puts on her spell-voice)
                Grey stones in the ditch,
                Red bricks on the ground,
                Build me my castle,
                Safe and sound.

Bricks and Stones rise again. Then the Wizard repeats his spell, and they fall down. Then the Witch repeats her spell, and they rise again. Finally the Wizard says very loudly :

Wizard :   Grey stones from the country,
               Red bricks from the town,
               Abra-cadabra!
               All fall down—
               And never stand again!

Bricks and Stones fall down for the last time.

Witch :   My spell has been broken,
               My charms are all done.
Boy :   The Witch has been beaten,
Girl :   The Wizard has won.

The Girl is free, and steps forward. The Wizard turns to the Witch.

Wizard :   Because you've done this,
               And because you've done that,
               You shall become . . .

                        (thinks hard)

               A lean black cat!

The Witch goes on all fours, and begins to hiss. Boy, Girl and Wizard chase her off, right. The Tree and the heaps of Stones and Bricks are left quietly to themselves again.

Tree:	Green leaves are swaying
	Like waves of the sea.
Upper Tree:	We are the branches,
Lower Tree:	And we are the tree.

Tree:	Cool, shady branches;
	Strong, sturdy tree.
Lower Tree:	Leaves at the top—tell us,
	What can you see?

Upper Tree:	We see a green hillside:
	It stands there alone
	With a heap of red brick,
	And a hump of grey stone.
Tree:	Just a heap of red brick,
	And a hump of grey stone.

Clive Sansom

A small charge is made for performances of this play to which the public is admitted. Application should be made to A. & C. Black Ltd, 35 Bedford Row, London WC1R 4JH

PART 2

Catch-Rhymes

Can your actions fit the words?

I

Up the road and down the road,
    and up the road again,
All across the meadow-lot
    and through the shady lane.
Skipping through the valley,
    so merrily we come,
Down the road and up the road,
    and here we are at home!

Traditional

2

Charley Marley
Stole some barley
Out of the baker's shop.
    The baker came out
    And gave him a clout,
Which made poor Charley hop.

Traditional

3

Left, right; left, right,
The regiment is coming;
Rum, tum, tum,
There's a drummer at the head.
Rum, tum, tum,
You can hear the drummer drumming
To the left, right, left,
Of the regimental tread.

Hilda Adams

4

GO, my little little boat,
ROW, my little little boat,
FLOW on the stream of the tide.

HI! my little little boat,
TRY, my little little boat,
FLY on the stream of the tide.

ROAM, my little little boat,
COME, my little little boat,
HOME on the stream of the tide.

Clive Sansom

The Hare

Between the valley and the hill
There sat a little hare;
It nibbled at the grass until
The ground was nearly bare.

And when the ground was nearly bare,
It rested in the sun;
A hunter came and saw it there
And shot it with his gun.

It thought it must be dead, be dead,
But, wonderful to say,
It found it was alive instead
And quickly ran away.

Translated from the German
by Rose Fyleman

Meeting

I came through the town to school today,
And who do you think I met on the way?
  An animal?
No.
  A person?
Yes.
  Then act this person and let us guess.

Noah's Ark

Noah called out to the beasts of the jungle:
    "It's going to rain like fun!
Look at the clouds there, look at the sky,
    And look at that fiery sun!

"Hurry aboard while there's time, me lads.
    There's room for the kangaroo,
The mouse and the moose, the elk and the
       elephant,
    Walk up two by two!"

So along came a great procession of
       animals,
    The grandest ever seen,
With two at the front of it, two at the back,
    And a hundred twos between.

They walked and they hopped and they
       trotted up the gangway.
    "Welcome, girls and boys!
You'll find all the food and the fodder
       you need
    —But don't make too much noise!"

Clive Sansom

Old Mother Chittle-Chattle

Old Mother Chittle-Chattle jumped
    out of bed
And out of the window she popped
    her head.
"The house is on fire, the grey goose
    is dead,
And the fox is come to town, O!"

Tinker, Tailor

"Tinker, tailor, soldier, sailor,
Rich man, poor man, beggar-man,
    thief."
If you could choose to be any of these,
Which would you choose to be?

I'd be a tinker, a travelling man,
To make you a kettle or mend you a pan.

I'd be a tailor, with needle and thread,
Bringing coats for your back and a hat
    for your head.

Can you go on?

When I was a Lady

When I was a lady,
A lady, a lady,
When I was a lady,
This is how I went . . .

When I was a farmer,
A farmer, a farmer,
When I was a farmer,
This is how I went . . .

When I was a princess,
A princess, a princess,
When I was a princess,
This is how I went . . .

Wiltshire folk-rhyme

Crossing the Stream

Step across by stepping-stones;
Lightly step from stone to stone.
Large stone to small stone,
Flat stone to round stone;
Step upon them, one by one,
Until you're safely over.

Clive Sansom

The Busy Housewives

Step out with your foot,
 step out with your shoe,
And see what the busy housewives do.
They wash, they wash,
 the whole day through.

Step out with your foot,
 step out with your shoe,
And see what the busy housewives do.
They starch, they starch,
 the whole day through.

Step out with your foot,
 step out with your shoe,
And see what the busy housewives do.
They peg, they peg,
 the whole day through.

Step out with your foot,
 step out with your shoe,
And see what the busy housewives do.
They iron, they iron,
 the whole day through.

Step out with your foot,
    step out with your shoe,
And see what the busy housewives do.
They eat, they eat,
    the whole day through.

Step out with your foot,
    step out with your shoe,
And see what the busy housewives do.
They drink, they drink,
    the whole day through.

Step out with your foot,
    step out with your shoe,
And see what the busy housewives do.
They gossip, they gossip,
    the whole day through.

Swiss rhyme translated by
Clive Sansom

Tell Me How I'm Walking

Walking, walking,
Tell me how I'm walking.
Which word's the right word
To say how I'm walking?

Farmer Brown

Old Farmer Brown
  Is digging up potatoes,
Digging up potatoes
  With an old, old spade.

Old Farmer Brown
  Has a sack of potatoes,
And he's carrying them home
  To be weighed, weighed, weighed.

Hilda Adams

Shepherd

Shepherd, let your sheep run out.
I dare not.
Why not?
Because the wicked wolf's about.

The wicked wolf is caught at last
In iron bars that hold him fast
Between the moon and the sun.
Let your sheep run.

*Translated from the Dutch
by Rose Fyleman*

The Turnip

Mr Finney had a turnip
And it grew and it grew,
And it grew behind the barn,
And the turnip did no harm.

And it grew, and it grew
Till it could grow no taller,
And Mr Finney took it
And he put it in the cellar.

There it lay, there it lay
Till it began to rot,
And his daughter Lizzie took it
And she put it in the pot.

And she boiled it, and she boiled it
As long as she was able,
And his daughter Susie took it
And she put it on the table.

Mr Finney and his wife
Both sat down to sup,
And they ate, and they ate,
And they ate the turnip up!

Jonathan Bing Visits the King

Poor old Jonathan Bing
Went out in his carriage to visit the
    King,
But everyone pointed and said, "Look at
    that!
Jonathan Bing has forgotten his hat!"
(He'd forgotten his hat!)

Poor old Jonathan Bing
Went home and put on a new hat for the
    King,
But up by the palace a soldier said, "Hi!
You can't see the King: you've forgotten
    your tie!"
(He'd forgotten his tie!)

Poor old Jonathan Bing,
He put on a *beautiful* tie for the King,
But when he arrived an archbishop said,
    "Ho!
You can't come to court in pyjamas,
    you know!"

Poor old Jonathan Bing
Went home and addressed a short note
     to the King:
   "If you please will excuse me
   I won't come to tea;
   For home's the best place for
   All people like me!"

Beatrice Curtis Brown

In the Wood at Night

Walk this wood in the moonlight,
Steal from tree to tree;
Make no sound on the mossy ground,
No print for Them to see.

Stay from the pool of moonlight,
Stir no sheltering bird;
Keep to the shade of the leaf-hung glade,
With never a whispered word!

And should a companion sleep here,
Wake her! wake her!
Come in soon from the midnight moon
Lest a charm should take her.

Clive Sansom

The King's Spectacles

The King has lost his spectacles!
The court is in a flurry!
They're searching here,
They're searching there.
It's *such* a hurry burry!

Where can they be?
Where *can* they be?
We'll search throughout the land.
And he who finds my spectacles
Shall have my daughter's hand.

Then, father dear,
A boy is here:
His home is in a shack.
He often finds a needle
In his master's big haystack.

Then bring him in!
Yes, bring him in!
We'll bring him in, sir, now . . .
My Lord, your noble spectacles
Are on your noble brow!

We'll now proclaim through all the land,
This boy shall have my daughter's hand!

James Gibson

Knight and Lady

A knight and a lady
    Went riding one day
Far into the forest,
    Away, away.

"Fair knight," said the lady,
    "I pray, have a care.
This forest is evil:
    Beware, beware!"

A fiery red dragon
    They spied on the grass.
The lady wept sorely,
    "Alas! Alas!"

The knight slew the dragon,
    The lady was gay:
They rode on together,
    Away, away.

Author unknown

Maypole Dancing

Round the Maypole, tread, tread, tread.
See how your ribbons thread, thread,
  thread.
First to the left side, then turn right;
Keep on dancing till night, night, night!

Lace those ribbons above your head,
Green with yellow, and blue with red.
Lace them neatly, one, two, three—
Then turn around and set them free!

Round the Maypole, tread, tread, tread,
Free those ribbons above your head.
Turn to the left side, then turn right;
Keep on dancing and you'll . . . be . . .
  right!

Based on an old country rhyme

Harold

King Harold, King Harold,
    he ran out of town,
And hurried to Hastings
    to fight for his crown;
But an archer let fly,
    and King Harold fell down,
And King William the Conqueror
    put on his crown.

Eleanor Farjeon

The Feet of the Law

The policeman paces down the street,
    Left, right, left.
Calmly, firmly, fall his feet,
    Left, right, left.

But should a villain heave in sight,
    Left, right, left,
He might receive* a terrible fright,
    Left-right, left-right, left-right, left!

Clive Sansom

★Speed up from here

Trying on the Slipper

"There!" said Ugly Sister One.
"Perfect! The shoe is mine!"
—"Sorry," said the Chamberlain,
"*Your* fitting is a nine."

"See!" cried Ugly Sister Two,
"It fits me like a glove!"
—"Kindly put your heel inside
And give your foot a shove."

"Cinderella, step this way:
Overcome your shyness.
Yes! The golden slipper's yours.
Follow me . . . Your Highness."

Clive Sansom

Old Woman from the Wood

Here comes an old woman
From out of the wood.
What would you do for us,
Work if you could?
    I would do anything.
Anything?
    Anything!
Show us your anything
Just as you should.

Based on an old Dorset rhyme

Too Polite

Broad met Stout
At the gate, and each
Was too polite to brush past.
"After you!" said Broad.
"After you!" said Stout.
They got in a dither
And went through together
And both
        stuck
                fast.

Ian Serraillier

The Cat and the Mouse

The cattie sat in the kiln-ring[1]
    Spinning, spinning,
And by came a little wee mousie,
    Rinning, rinning.[2]

"I swept out my house this morning,
    My lonesome, lonesome lady."
"'Twas a sign you didn't sit among dirt,"
    Said she, said she.

"I found two pennies in it,
    My lonesome, lonesome lady."
"'Twas a sign that you weren't silverless,"
    Said she, said she.

"I bought a sheep's head with them,
    My lonesome, lonesome lady."
"'Twas a sign that you weren't kitchenless,"
    Said she, said she.

"I put it in the saucepan to boil,
    My lonesome, lonesome lady."
"'Twas a sign you didn't eat it raw,"
    Said she, said she.

"I put it in the window to cool,
    My lonesome, lonesome lady."
"'Twas a sign you didn't burn your
        tongue,"
    Said she, said she.

"By came a cattie who ate it,
    My lonesome, lonesome lady."
"And so will I you—worry, worry;
        gnash, gnash!"
    Said she, said she.

From a Scottish rhyme

¹ hearth   ² running

The Old Wives

Two old wives sat a-talking,
A-talking, a-talking, a-talking;
Two old wives sat a-talking
About the wind and weather—
Till their two old heads fell a-nodding,
A-nodding, a-nodding, a-nodding,
Till their two old heads fell a-nodding,
Their two old heads together.

The Proud Tower

Soldiers : Surrender, Tower; surrender!
           And let us march inside.
Tower :   Pass by, you foolish soldiers:
           Do not insult our pride.

Soldiers : We shall go and tell the Duke—
           He says this Tower must fall.
Tower :   Go and tell your noble Duke:
           You cannot climb the wall.

Soldiers march off to the Duke.

Soldiers : O royal Duke and captain,
           We kneel before thy power.
           Give us now an armèd guard
           To help us take the Tower.

Duke :   Go, my guard, and go, my son,
           So brave in battlefield.
           Pull the wall down, stone by stone
           This stubborn Tower must yield.

*Headed by Duke's son, Guard and
Soldiers march round the Tower.*

Soldiers : Surrender, Tower; surrender!
           And let us march inside.

Tower :   Welcome, you foolish soldiers:
          Our gates are open wide!

Translated by Mary Cousins

Danger: Witches at Work!

Take . . . take—
The tail of a snake,
The shell of a snail,
The fin of a whale,
A mastiff's growl,
The hoot of an owl,
The wing of a bat,
A wizard's hat,
The front-door mat!—
And after that
Stir them round,
Around and around,
To mix a stew
For the Witches' brew
For the charms we make
And the charms we break
In our magic store.
And spells galore!
And spells galore!!

Clive Sansom

The Magic Cloak

As he passes the townsfolk,
Cloak on arm,
No-one expresses
The least alarm.

But the cloak is an artful,
Magical cloak,
Woven at night
By the Secret Folk;

And now, without warning,
He twirls it on—
"Why, bless my buttons!
The boy has gone!"

He walks unseen
In his magic cloak.
"Who bumped me then?"
—"Who laughed?"—"Who spoke?"

They stare at the pavement,
Gape in the air.
Their eyes cannot spot the lad
Anywhere!

Some have been jostled,
Some take a fall;
Others are poked at by
Nothing at all—

Till the city gate,
To their great delight,
Creaks itself open
With no-one in sight,

And through the gap,
With a laugh and a shout,
Artfully, magically,
No-one goes out!

Clive Sansom

Laburnum Walk

As we went down Laburnum Walk,
We met a man who couldn't talk.
He couldn't say a single word,
But everything he said, we heard!
　　He went like this, he went like that—
　　Now what do you think he said?

American rhyme

The Three Dukes

Here come three dukes a-riding,
    A-riding, a-riding;
Here come three dukes a-riding,
    With a rancy, tancy, tay!

And what is your goodwill, sirs?
    Goodwill, sirs? goodwill, sirs?
And what is your goodwill, sirs,
    With a rancy, tancy, tay?

Our goodwill is to marry,
    To marry, to marry,
Our goodwill is to marry,
    With a rancy, tancy, tay!

Then marry with my daughters,
    My daughters, my daughters,
Then marry with my daughters,
    With a rancy, tancy, tay!

They're all as stiff as pokers,
    As pokers, as pokers,
They're all as stiff as pokers,
    With a rancy, tancy, tay!

They are far too good for you, sirs,
    For you, sirs; for you, sirs;
They are far too good for you, sirs,
    With a rancy, tancy, tay!

So they turned and rode them westward,
    Westward, westward,
They turned and rode them westward,
    With a rancy, tancy, tay!

Based on a West Country rhyme

The Recruiting Sergeant

Come here to me, my merry, merry men!
    Said a sergeant at the fair;
And the bumpkins all were very merry men
    And they all came running there.
Fat and spare, round and square,
    See them stare with noddles bare,
And the piper piped an air,
    And the drummer drummed his share
With a rub-a-dub, rub-a-dub, row dow
      dow,
And the little dogs answered bow, wow,
      wow,
    And the boys cried out Hurrah!
    Hurrah! Hurrah! Hurrah!

King Alfred

Those taking part :

Alfred   Peasant
Courtiers   Peasant's Wife
Chorus

There is a chair at the back of the stage or acting-space, near the centre. King Alfred is seated on this, with his Courtiers at each side. The Chorus stands behind.

Chorus :   King Alfred, King Alfred,
              Afterwards 'the Great',
              Laid aside his golden crown
              And his sword of state.

Alfred :   Take my sword, take my crown,
              They're no use to me.
              Till my kingdom is my own
              A peasant I shall be.

Chorus :   Peasant's dress, peasant's cloak,
              These he wore instead,
              With a simple peasant's hat
              As crown on his head.

Alfred : Through moorland, through
      marshes
    I will track the Dane.
    Keep my golden crown and
      sword
    Till I come again.

The Courtiers disperse. Alfred walks round the front of the acting-space to the back and then stops at an imaginary door on the right.

Chorus : King Alfred, King Alfred,
    Tramped through marsh and
      moor,
    Until he found a wattle hut
    And knocked at the door.

Peasant's Wife comes in from left.

Wife : What man knocks? what man
     calls?
    A Saxon or a Dane?

Alfred : A true Saxon's waiting here
    To shelter from the rain.

Wife: Bad weather, bad weather,
For trudging in the mire.
Come inside, my Saxon,
And dry at the fire.

Sit down, man! sit down there!
Your keep you shall earn.
Watch these cakes baking,
And see they don't burn.

Alfred sits on the chair. The Wife goes out, left. There is a silence while Alfred tries hard to keep awake, but finally falls asleep. Then the Chorus speaks:

Chorus: King Alfred, King Alfred—
King Alfred fell asleep!
Listen to the snoring,
Long and loud and deep . . .

Peasant's Wife returns and starts beating him.

Wife: You ruffian! you rascal!
Can't you keep awake?
See what you have done there—
Burned every cake!

Peasant enters from left, and stops her.

Peasant : Hold your hand, hold your stick,
Stop your chattering!
This man is no peasant,
But our lord, the King.

Wife : My goodness! my gracious!
What shall I do?
Forgive me, Your Majesty—
And I'll forgive you.

Short tableau. Then Peasant and Wife step aside, while Alfred moves to the back.

Chorus : King Alfred, King Alfred,
Went to fight the Dane,
Drove him from the kingdom,
Then came home again.

The Courtiers enter and welcome Alfred as he turns round and moves towards the front again.

Alfred : Peasant's hat, peasant's cloak,
I fling them to the floor.
Bring my sword and golden crown:
I am King once more!

Alfred sits on the chair. The Courtiers crown him.

Chorus : The great sword, the state sword
They buckled on instead,
And the crown of beaten gold
Placed on his head.

His vassals, his nobles,
They throned him in state—
All : King Alfred, King Alfred,
King Alfred the Great!

Clive Sansom

A small charge is made for performances of this play to which the public is admitted. Application should be made to A. & C. Black Ltd, 35 Bedford Row, London WC1R 4JH

Jock McGregor

When Jock sets out for the Western Isles,
   His tartan kilt a-swinging,
He proudly fills the Scottish hills
   With loud and joyful singing:
      "Och, ay!
      We're awa' to Skye!"

When Jock comes back from the Western
   Isles,
   His very bones are groaning.
With aching head and feet like lead,
   He stumbles homeward, moaning:
      "Hoots! toots!
      These are awfu' boots!"

Clive Sansom

Catch-Rhymes

1

Left . . . left,
Left, right, left.
Left . . . left,
Left, right, left.
If . . . wrong
You must chànge yòur stèp.
Left . . . left,
Left, right, left.

2

Strong is our arm
And heavy we can strike,
With a bang on the hammer
And a clang on the spike.

3

Swing the long scythe
    through the flowering grass;
See the stalks falling
    in swathes as we pass.
Curved is its blade
    like the curve of the moon,
Scything and swinging
    the whole afternoon.

Clive Sansom

A Yankee ship came down the river,
  Blow, boys, blow.
A Yankee ship came down the river,
  Blow, my bully boys, blow!

And who do you think was skipper of her?
  Blow, boys, blow.
Dandy Jim from old Carolina,
  Blow, my bully boys, blow!

And what do you think they had for
    dinner?
  Blow, boys, blow.
Monkey's lights and donkey's liver,
  Blow, my bully boys, blow!

And what do you think they had for
    supper?
  Blow, boys, blow.
Hard tack and Yankee leather,
  Blow, my bully boys, blow!

Then blow, my boys, and blow together,
  Blow, boys, blow.
Blow, my boys, for better weather,
  Blow, my bully boys, blow!

American sea-shanty

Statues

Dancer, dancer, moving there,
Moving, miming everywhere,
Acting, playing, as you will—
Dancer, dancer, stand quite STILL!

Statue, statue, standing there,
Motionless, and light as air,
Far removed from thoughts of men—
Statue, statue, LIVE again!

Mr Tom Narrow

A scandalous man
    Was Mr Tom Narrow,
He pushed his grandmother
    Round in a barrow.
And he called out loud
    As he rang his bell,
"Grannies to sell!
    Old Grannies to sell!"

The neighbours said,
    As he passed them by,
"This poor old lady
    We will not buy.
He surely must be
    A mischievous man
To try for to sell
    His own dear Gran."

"Besides," said another,
    "If you ask me,
She'd be very small use
    That I can see."
"You're right," said a third,
    "And no mistake—
A very poor bargain
    She'd surely make."

So Mr Tom Narrow
    He scratched his head,
And he sent his grandmother
    Back to bed;
And he rang his bell
    Through all the town
Till he sold his barrow
    For half a crown.

James Reeves

The Street-Sellers

Visitor : Good evening, sir. Is this London
    Town?

Londoner : Yes. Can I help you?

Visitor : Well, sir, it's like this. I've come
    to buy some goods, but I don't know
    where to look for them.

Londoner : In London, you don't have to
    look for them. Just stand here, and
    the goods will come to you. Listen!

Muffin Man
Muffins O! Crumpets O!
Come buy, come buy from me.
Muffins and crumpets! Muffins O!
For breakfast and for tea.

Quack
Clove water, stomach water!
Clove water, stomach water!

Ballad-Seller
You maidens and men,
Come buy what you lack—
Come buy the fair ballads
I have in my pack.

Herb-Seller
All a-growing,
All a-blowing.
Rue, sage and mint,
A farthing a bunch!

Mousetrap-Seller
Buy a mousetrap, a mousetrap,
Or a tormentor for your fleas!

Pudding-Seller
Who wants some pudding, nice and hot?
  Now is the time to try it.
Just taken from the smoking pot—
  And taste before you buy it.

Milk-Seller
Rain, frost or snow, or hot or cold,
  I travel up and down.
The cream and milk you buy from me
  Is best in all the town.

Cane-Seller
Buy a cane for naughty boys!
Buy a cane for naughty boys!

Glass-Seller

Glasses, glasses, fine glasses buy!
Fine Venice glasses—no crystal more clear
Of all forms and fashions, buy glasses here
Glasses, glasses, fine glasses I cry.
Come, buy them quickly, before I pass by.

Londoner : Well, those are some of the
goods for sale. Which will you choose?
Visitor : There are far too many things. I
can't make up my mind.

Voice in distance : "Past nine o'clock!"

Londoner : Past nine o'clock. It's too late
for trading now. Come home with me
for the night, and start your buying in
the morning.
Visitor : Thank you. That is very kind of
you.

They leave. Bellman enters.

Bellman

Give care to your clocks!
Beware your locks,
Your fire and your light!

And God give you goodnight!
Past nine o'clock!

> (*He leaves.*)

Past nine o'clock!

*Traditional street-cries
arranged by Clive Sansom*

The Old Steam-Train

Down goes the signal. "All aboard
    the puff-puff!"
Jànga-langa, jànga-langa-làng goes
    the bell and
People come a-hurrying, and bang go
    the doors and
Click! go the keys as they lock 'em up
    well, and
Feee! goes the whistle, and waggle goes
    the flag, and
Ooo! says the engine, choo-choo-chof,
Choo—rumble—rumble—rumble—
    choo—rumble, rumble, rumble,
Rattle—bump—rumble as the train
    moves off.

Author unknown

Overheard on a Saltmarsh

Nymph! nymph! what are your beads?
Green glass, Goblin. Why do you stare at
    them?
Give them me.
              No.
Give them me. Give them me.
              No.
Then I will howl all night in the reeds,
Lie in the mud and howl for them.

Goblin, why do you love them so?

They are better than stars or water,
Better than voices of winds that sing,
Better than any man's fair daughter,
Your green glass beads on a silver ring.

Hush, I stole them out of the moon.

Give me your beads, I desire them.
              No.
I will howl in a deep lagoon
For your green glass beads, I love them so.
Give them me. Give them.
              No.

Harold Monro

Clown

With his baggy pants
And blue umbrella
He looks such a quizzical,
Comical fella.

Walking the tightrope
High in the air,
Look at him balancing,
Tottering there!

Two steps forward,
One step back—
If he's not careful
He'll come down smack.

A lurch to the left,
A lunge to the right,
He stumbles, staggers . . .
Oh, what a fright!

Then—
Shuffle-wobble, dither-wobble,
Slide and glide—
He lands up safe
On the other side!

Clive Sansom

London Wall

A Roman built up London Wall
    With his big bricks and his little bricks,
A Roman built up London Wall
With its straw and its lime and its mortar
    and all.

Then he stood on the top, so stalwart
    and tall,
    On the big bricks and the little bricks,
He stood on the top, so stalwart and tall,
With his spear and his shield and his
    helmet and all.

He looked down on London, all bustle
    and brawl,
    And big bricks and little bricks,
He looked down on London, all bustle
    and brawl,
With its streets and its chimneys and
    markets and all—

With its mansions, its rivers, its parks
    and Whitehall,
    And its big bricks and its little bricks,

With its mansions, its rivers, its parks
    and Whitehall,
Its prisons, its churches, its Tower
    and St Paul.

"I've built up a Wall that never can fall,
   With my big bricks and my little bricks,
I've built up a Wall that never can fall
By cannon, or thunder, or earthquake
    and all!"

But London laughed low, and began
    for to crawl
   Through the big bricks and the little
    bricks,
London laughed low, and began for to
    crawl
To the North, to the West, to the South,
    East and all.

There came a great crack in the side of
    the Wall,
   In the big bricks and the little bricks,
There came a great crack in the side of
    the Wall,
And down fell the Wall and the Roman
    and all!

Eleanor Farjeon

Guessing a Rhyme

What is this rhyme?
Oh, what is this rhyme?
We'll spell it in action
And tell it in mime.
See if you guess it
The very first time.

The Ballad of John Blunt

Mr John Blunt, he sat in a chair,
As he'd often done before, O.
But one thing he forgot to do,
Which was to bar the door, O.

"I am old, and the wind is cold,
It blows across the floor, O.
Mrs John Blunt, you're younger than I—
Get up and bar the door, O."

"A bargain, a bargain I'll make, my man,
A bargain I'll make to be sure, O,
That whoever speaks the very first word
Shall get up and bar the door, O!"

There came three travellers travelling
     by,
And they travelled across the moor, O.
But never a house did those three find
Till they came to John Blunt's door, O.

They ate up his victuals, they drank up
     his drink,
And then they called for more, O.
But never a word did the old man speak
For fear of barring the door, O.

They pulled the old woman from out of
     her chair,
They rolled her along the floor, O.
But never a word did the woman speak
For fear of barring the door, O.

"You've eaten my victuals, and drunk
     up my drink,
And you've rolled my wife on the floor,
     O."
"Ah, Mr John Blunt, you've spoken the
     word—
Get up and bar the door, O!"

King John

John was a tyrant,
John was a tartar,
But John put his name to the Great Big
  Charter.
Every baron
From Thames to Tweed,
Followed the road
To Runnymede.
Every baron had something to say
To poor perplexed King John that day.
"Pray sign your name," said Guy de
  Gaunt;
"It's easily done, and it's all we want."
"A J and an O and an H and an N,"
Said Hugo, Baron of Harpenden.
Quietly spoke the Lord Rambure:
"Oblige, Lord King, with your signature."
"Your name, my liege, to be writ just here
A mere formality," laughed de Bere.
"A stroke of the pen and the thing is done,
Murmured Sir Roger of Trumpington.
"Done in a twinkling," sniffed de Guise.
Said Stephen Langton: "Sign, *if* you
  please!"

So many people
Egging him on,
I can't help feeling
Sorry for John.

Hugh Chesterman

Bell-Ringing

Up in the bell-loft
   Great Tom is ringing—
Under the cross-beams
   Clanging and swinging.

Cottage and farmstead
   Wake to his tolling,
Over the cornfields
   Booming and rolling.

The rope carries roofwards, till
   Pulled by the ringer;
Drawn up by the bell-weight, then
   Down he will bring her.

In the dark bell-loft
   Great Tom is chiming;
Sunrise and eve-tide
   Pass to his timing.

Clive Sansom

The Three Tinkers

We are three tinkers, and here we stand
Waiting to ask for your daughters' hand.
Oh, may we have lodgings here, oh here?
May we have lodgings here?

(Sleep, my daughters, do not wake,
Here come three tinkers we cannot take.)
We have no lodgings here, oh here;
We have no lodgings here.

We are three tailors, and here we stand
Waiting to ask for your daughters' hand.
Oh, may we have lodgings here, oh here?
May we have lodgings here?

(Sleep, my daughters, do not wake,
Here come three tailors we cannot take.)
We have no lodgings here, oh here;
We have no lodgings here.

We are three soldiers, and here we stand
Waiting to ask for your daughters' hand.
Oh, may we have lodgings here, oh here?
May we have lodgings here?

(Sleep, my daughters, do not wake,
Here come three soldiers we cannot take.)
We have no lodgings here, oh here;
We have no lodgings here.

We are three sailors, and here we stand
Waiting to ask for your daughters' hand.
Oh, may we have lodgings here, oh here?
May we have lodgings here?

(Sleep, my daughters, do not wake.
Here come three sailors we cannot take.)
We have no lodgings here, oh here;
We have no lodgings here.

We are three kings, and here we stand
Waiting to ask for your daughters' hand.
Oh, may we have lodgings here, oh here?
May we have lodgings here?

(Wake, my daughters, do not sleep!
Here come three kings that we can keep.)
Yes, we have lodgings here, oh here;
We have some lodgings here!

Adapted from an old North Country rhyme

Going to the Fair

"Here I come trudging to Camperdown
    Fair
With a piebald horse and a dove-grey
    mare.
[Come along, everyone! Who'd like a
    horse with one eye?"]*

"Here I come trundling to Camperdown
    Fair.
Who'll buy an apple, a peach or a pear?"

"Here I come tramping to Camperdown
    Fair.
I'll mend your table or cane your chair."

"Here I come traipsing to Camperdown
    Fair,
With ribbons for ladies and bangles
    to wear."

"Here I come strolling to Camperdown
    Fair.
Shall I shave your whiskers or cut your
    hair?"

*see page 120

There was a King

There was a king came riding by
    In panoply and state;
There was a ragged beggar-man
    A-begging at his gate.

The king he saw the beggar-man,
    The king he stopped and said
(A-sighing as he said it and
    A-shaking of his head):

"O beggar-man, O beggar-man!
    If people only knew
How willingly, how willingly
    I'd change my state with you."

This caused the lords to wonder,
    Who followed in his train:
But the beggar went on begging,
    And the king rode on again.

Emile Jacot

Bad Sir Brian Botany

Sir Brian had a battleaxe with great big
    knobs on;
  He went among the villagers and
    blipped them on the head.
On Wednesday and on Saturday, but
    mostly on the latter day,
  He called at all the cottages, and this
    is what he said:
"I am Sir Brian!" (*ting-ling*)
  "I am Sir Brian!" (*rat-tat*)
"I am Sir Brian, as bold as a lion—
  Take *that!*—and *that!*—and *that!*"

Sir Brian had a pair of boots with great
    big spurs on,
  A fighting pair of which he was
    particularly fond.
On Tuesday and on Friday, just to make
    the street look tidy,
  He'd collect the passing villagers
    and kick them in the pond.
"I am Sir Brian!" (*sper-lash!*)
  "I am Sir Brian!" (*sper-losh!*)
"I am Sir Brian, as bold as a lion—
  Is there anyone else for a wash?"

Sir Brian woke one morning, and he
    couldn't find his battleaxe;
  He walked into the village in his second
    pair of boots.
He had gone a hundred paces, when the
    street was full of faces,
  And the villagers were round him with
    ironical salutes:
  "You are Sir Brian? Indeed!
    You are Sir Brian? Dear, dear!
  You are Sir Brian, as bold as a lion?
    Delighted to meet you here!"

Sir Brian went a journey, and he found
    a lot of duck-weed;
  They pulled him out and dried him,
    and they blipped *him* on the head.
They took him by the breeches, and they
    hurled him into ditches,
  And they pushed him under waterfalls,
    and this is what they said:
  "You are Sir Brian—don't laugh,
    You are Sir Brian—don't cry,
  You are Sir Brian, as bold as a lion—
    Sir Brian, the lion, goodbye!"

Sir Brian struggled home again, and
　　　chopped up his battleaxe,
　　Sir Brian took his fighting boots, and
　　　threw them in the fire.
He is quite a different person now he
　　　hasn't got his spurs on,
　　And he goes about the village as
　　　B. Botany, Esquire.
　　"I am Sir Brian? Oh *no!*
　　　I am Sir Brian? Who's he?
　　I haven't got any title. I'm Botany—
　　　Plain Mr Botany (B)."

A. A. Milne

Earl Haldan's Daughter

It was Earl Haldan's daughter;
She looked across the sea,
She looked across the water
And long and loud laughed she:
"The locks of six princesses
Must be my marriage-fee,
So hey, bonny boat, and ho, bonny boat!
Who comes a-wooing me?"

It was Earl Haldan's daughter;
She walked along the strand
When she was aware of a knight so fair
Come sailing to the land.
His sails were all of velvet,
His masts of beaten gold.
"Hey, bonny boat, and ho, bonny boat!
Who saileth here so bold?"

"The locks of five princesses
I won beyond the sea;
I clipped their golden tresses
To fringe a cloak for thee.
One handful yet is wanting,
But one of all the tale;
So hey, bonny boat, and ho, bonny boat!
Furl up thy velvet sail!"

He leapt into the water,
That rover young and bold;
He gripped Earl Haldan's daughter,
He clipped her locks of gold.
"Go weep, go weep, proud maiden,
The tale is full today.
Now hey, bonny boat, and ho, bonny boat!
Sail Westward ho! away!"

Charles Kingsley

The Saucy Sailor

"Come, my own one; come, my fond one,
　Come, my dearest, unto me.
Will you wed with a poor sailor lad
　Who has just returned from sea?"

"O indeed, I'll have no sailor,
　For he's dirty, smells of tar.
You are ragged, you are saucy—
　Get you gone, you Jacky Tar!"

"If I'm dirty, if I'm ragged,
　If, maybe, of tar I smell,
Yet I've silver in my pocket
　And a store of gold as well."

"Indeed, sir, I was joking—
　I am quite beneath your spell.
Ragged, dirty, tarry sailors
　I love more than words can tell."

"Do you take me to be foolish,
　Do you think that I am mad?—
That I'd wed the like of you, miss,
　When there's others to be had?

"No, I'll cross the briny ocean,
   No, my boat shall spread her wing.
You refused me, ragged, dirty—
   Not for you the wedding ring!"

English folk-song

Sink Song

Scouring out the porridge pot,
   Round and round and round!

Out with all the scraith and scoopery,
Lift the eely ooly droopery,
Chase the glubbery slubbery gloopery,
   Round and round and round!

Out with all the doleful dithery,
Ladle out the slimy slithery,
Hunt and catch the hithery thithery,
   Round and round and round!

Out with all the obbly gubbly,
On the stove it burns so bubbly,
Use the spoon and use it doubly,
   Round and round and round!

J. A. Lindon

Young Eagle-Feather

First he took his bow for hunting
(Strong, yet supple as a willow)
Stretched the string, and plucked it
    lightly,
Knowing that the bow was worthy,
Knowing that its craft would serve him.
    Next, from out a store of arrows,
Each one keen and plumed with feathers,
Chose the best and filled the quiver
That was slung across his shoulder;
Then he left his camp at sunrise,
While his friends and braves were
    sleeping,
To hunt the wild deer in the forest.
    Like a deer himself, his footsteps
Made no stir in leaves or branches,
Left no track or spoor behind him.
So he journeyed through the forest,
Swift yet cautious, calm yet watchful,
Nose and ears and eyes alerted
For any scent or sound or movement.
    Suddenly he stopped and straightened;
Like a tree he stood, unmoving,
Like a rooted tree he waited.

Near, within a narrow clearing,
Stood a deer, his head uplifted,
Tense and wary, poised for action.
   Eagle-Feather watched and waited,
While the deer still paused uncertain,
Sniffed the morning air for danger;
Then relaxed, returned to grazing.
Silently he slipped an arrow;
Brought it softly to the bow-string;
Slowly raised the bow before him;
Felt the tension in the bow-string;
Loosed the shaft . . .
   The deer had vanished!

Clive Sansom

The Revolving Door

Don't go through that revolving door!
Why not?
My father's in it.
Who's your father?
McGillacuddy.
What! That's *my* name.
Father!
Son!

American patter-game

The Dragon

Oh, once there was a dragon,
A green and spiky dragon;
Once there was a dragon
Who lived in old Japan.

His home was in a cavern,
A green and slimy cavern;
His home was in a cavern
Where a shiny river ran.

One day he went out hunting
In a dark and shadowy forest;
One day he went out hunting,
And so his day began.

He met a knight in armour,
In bright and shining armour;
He met a knight in armour,
A brave, gallant man.

The trees called out a warning:
"Beware, sir! beware, sir!"
The trees called out a warning,
And so he changed his plan.

They heard a mighty crashing,
A slashing, a clashing;
They heard a mighty crashing:
"Kill him if you can!"

The dragon roared in anger,
He tossed his head in fury;
The dragon roared in anger,
Flashed his tail—and ran!

The knight he chased and slew him,
That green and spiky dragon;
The knight he chased and slew him,
The last of all his clan.

And then he rode on bravely,
And waved his sword above him.
The trees all tossed their branches:
"Hurrah for old Japan!"

Author unknown

FOUR CHARACTERS

1 The Pirate Chief

One-eyed Jack, the pirate chief,
Was a terrible, fearsome ocean thief.
　　He wore a peg
　　Upon one leg;
　　He wore a hook
　　And a dirty look.
One-eyed Jack, the pirate chief,
A terrible, fearsome ocean thief.

Author unknown

2 Fried-Fish Seller

Try me potatoes and me 'ot fried fish!
You can 'ave a taster of 'em if you wish.
You can eat 'em 'ere on a plate or a dish,
Or take 'em in a little bit o' paper!

London song

3 Railway Navvy

I'm a navvy, you're a navvy,
Working on the line.
Five-and-twenty bob a week
And all the overtime.
Roast beef, boiled beef,
Puddings made of eggs—
Up jumps a navvy
With a pair of sausage legs!

Author unknown

4 The Wicked Burglar

Forth from his den to steal he stole,
His bags of chink he chunk,
And many a wicked smile he smole,
And many a wink he wunk.

Author unknown

King Canute

Those taking part :

Canute Courtiers

Chamberlain Crowd

Chorus

Scene : The sea-shore. There is a small platform at the back of the stage or acting-space, centre; and a deck-chair towards the front, left of centre. The Chorus stands to the right.

Chorus :

On a sunny day
In early May,
One thousand and thirty-three,
King Canute
Took his bathing-suit
And came down to the sea.

Canute enters, followed at a respectful distance by his Courtiers. He puts a toe in the sea, which is at the very front of the acting-space.

The sea was cold,
The King was old;
He very soon changed his mind,
And he sat down there
On an old deck-chair:
His courtiers stood behind.

He does. They do.

Canute :

Although I'm King,
Not a single thing
Is ever done to please me.
My bath was not
What I'd call hot,
And now you try to freeze me!

Courtiers :

It is not we,
Your Majesty.
The fault it is the sea's.

Chamberlain :

I told it precisely
To heat itself nicely
To sixty-five degrees.

If it declines
Though the sun still shines,
The remedy, Sire, is yours.
Speak to it strongly
For acting so wrongly,
And banish it from your shores.

Canute :

Thank you, my man,
An excellent plan.
I'll show it I'm not afraid.
A king should swim
When it pleases him
And never be disobeyed.

*He gets up from his chair, comes to the
front, and calls out loudly across the
audience.*

Sea! North Sea!
Just listen to me!
My orders are firm and plain.
You will leave this beach
At the end of my speech
And never return again!

*Courtiers await events with great interest.
Other people enter, and look on from a
distance.*

Chorus :

From far and wide
They watched the tide
To see the retreat begin,
And got ready to shout
As the sea moved out—
But still the sea moved in!

To their distress,
Instead of less,
The water grew more and more;
And they saw it expand
Across the sand
The whole length of the shore.

The sea crept on
Till the beach had gone,
And trickled around his toes.
But there he stood
Like a block of wood
As the water rose and rose.

Courtiers retire towards platform.

Courtiers :

O King, we beseech,
Repeat your speech!
The sea could not have heard.

Chorus :

But stern and mute
Stood King Canute,
Refusing to say a word.

*Courtiers get on to platform, and whisper
together.*

Courtiers :

(The sea is too cold
For a bathe, we're told,
But now he will have to wade.)
The water, Sire,
Gets higher and higher;
Won't you walk on the esplanade?

Chorus :

He turned not round,
Nor uttered a sound—
Except for a double sneeze.

(like this)

He refused to say
That he'd lost the day,
Though the sea was around his knees.

And then at last,
As it rolled in fast
And his courtiers watched from the pier
His Majesty felt
It reach to his belt,
And he shouted loud and clear:

Canute :

Sea! North Sea!
Just listen to me!
My orders are firm and plain.
   Come right in-shore
   As you have before,
And *then* go out again.

Chorus :

The men on the pier
Raised cheer on cheer,
(It was marvellous to behold them)
   While the waves came in—
   AND IN—AND IN—-
Exactly as he told them!

He turned and bowed
To the cheering crowd,
With a damp yet royal grace.
   He had disappeared
   Right up to his beard
But, at least—he'd saved his face!

So let us salute
Good King Canute—
Though while we praise his endeavour,
Kings may come, we know,
And kings may go,
But the sea goes on for ever.

Clive Sansom

A small charge is made for performances of this play to which
the public is admitted. Application should be made to

A. & C. Black Ltd, 35 Bedford Row, London WC1R 4JH

CHILDREN AND RHYME

In education we sometimes find it difficult to adopt a new idea without discarding an old one. We insist on Either/Or. So the growth of free drama, which has revitalised the work in schools, has led some of its exponents to reject everything that is ready-made—including rhymes like these. One writer has branded all rhyme as 'unnatural' for children, something foisted on them by reactionary adults.

This seems to be distorting facts to fit a theory. Babies of a few months old are pleased by matching sounds; and though grown-ups may be at fault in perpetuating 'gee-gee' and 'bow-wow', I doubt if they originally coined these words. Later, when a child begins to talk and to enjoy talking, he takes to rhyme as eagerly as a duckling to water. And not only rhymes, but puns and nonsense words. They are part of his delight in sounds and rhythms—something which many adults have lost, but which is at the heart of language appreciation.

That, and not an adult conspiracy, accounts for the pleasure children still take in nursery rhymes, weather rhymes, play rhymes and all the other verses which have survived in their thousands. If anyone questions the 'thousands', he should flex his muscles and take down the massive collections made by Iona and Peter Opie. They are part of a literary heritage which cannot be ignored without impoverishing our language and ourselves.

Nor is rhyme-making a thing of the past. The tradition is being continued by children in street and playground as part of their tribal lore. Few of these rhymes suggest coercion or a grown-up's helping hand. As for 'unnaturalness', this is what the Opies say:

> Rhyme seems to appeal to a child as something funny and remark-able in itself . . . Listening to children as they "tumble and rhyme" out of school (as Dylan Thomas described them) they seem to have a chant on their lips as constantly as they have a comic in their hands or a sweet in their mouths.

In fact the authors regard rhymes as a natural stage in language development and part of a child's introduction to life.

Of course he *is* affected by adult examples. But the child is able to add his own personality, his sense of humour, and his sheer love of words:

> Good King Wenceslas went out
> In the kitchen garden,
> Bumped into a brussels sprout
> And said, "I beg your pardon."

I agree that children's compositions should not be confined to rhymes. When they want to express their deepest feelings (writing out of their private rather than their public selves) they are usually most successful in free verse. This is partly because, at the Primary stage, they lack the word-store and technical control needed to handle rhyme in serious situations. But why should they be denied the pleasure of speaking these rhymes? There is no reason why rhyme and free drama should not live happily together, one enlivening the other.

HOW TO USE THE RHYMES

These rhymes may be treated in several ways:

Some, entirely in dialogue, are spoken by the characters themselves.

Some are spoken by a narrator (or preferably a narrative group) while the characters mime the action.

Some are partly told, partly acted.

Others are spoken first and acted afterwards.

They are essentially *oral* rhymes: the best introduction is for them to be said to the children. If children read a rhyme from print, without having heard it first, their speaking is likely to be stiff or sing-song.

With certain rhymes (e.g. "Giant", p 5) the teacher should continue to say the narrative lines on several occasions, or it will be difficult for those who are miming. And even then it may be advisable for a group to speak *with* the teacher before taking over from her. In simpler rhymes they can take straight over. Much depends on the rhyme itself and the children's experience. In the early stages it may be necessary for the whole class to work together under the teacher's direction—some speaking; some acting or miming; some watching, listening and joining in discussion. Later, the class may be divided into separate groups, each group practising a rhyme by itself. See *Speech and Communication in the Primary School* (pp 81-90) for general suggestions on the Group Method in drama.

A story group should be small, so that the speaking is light and lively. Mass recitation by the whole class tends to be dull and heavy.

Where words and movements coincide (as in "Bell Ringing", p 89) the story group should not take an active part; otherwise the speaking becomes a jingle. Use two groups—one for speech, one for movement—and exchange them later.

Some rhymes (e.g. "Knight and Lady", p 55) contain tricky changes from narrative to dramatic speech:

> "Fair knight," said the lady,
> "I pray have a care."

It may seem logical for "said the lady" to be spoken by the story group, but this is seldom satisfactory in practice: several voices saying relatively unimportant words swamp the single voice saying important words. It is usually better for the character himself to say both parts.

The aim throughout is liveliness and spontaneity. Nothing should become 'set'. Each repetition is an opportunity for changes and for renewed vitality. There should be frequent discussions on characterisation, movement, etc. and individuality should be encouraged.

Suggestions on specific rhymes are confined to those which may present problems.

PART 1

5 GIANT The first two lines of each stanza are slow, strong and measured; the last two are light and quick.

7 RABBIT RHYMES 1 Rabbit is asleep in the centre of a ring of children. They close in, speaking their lines. "Oh, how still . . . Is he ill?" is spoken very softly.

8 CATCH-RHYMES Words and actions should synchronise exactly. After some straight practices, characterisation might be added. For further material see *Rhythm Rhymes*, edited by Ruth Sansom (Black).

10 GEESE One of many traditional excuses for chasing each other! See "Old Dame" (p 24) and "The Sheep and the Wolf" (p 26), and others in *Children's Games in Street and Playground*, edited by Iona and Peter Opie (Oxford).

11 GARDENING A different child speaks line 3, and then demonstrates. Precise miming should be encouraged. e.g. Digging: "How do you hold a spade?" Weeding: "What kind of weeds are they?" Wheelbarrow: "Is it full or empty?"

11 WHO'S THAT RINGING? Sometimes the next-to-the-last line reads: "For that's the way to cure a little *pussy*-cat", but very efficient speech is needed to keep the rhythm.

14 WHAT ARE YOU GOING TO BE? Follow lady and soldier with other people. It is surprising how even many-syllabled words can fit in: window-cleaner, lorry-driver, garage man, etc.

14 RIDING ON AN ENGINE Children in crocodile formation. One in front pulls an imaginary lever and they all move off, continuing after the words finish.

15 TALES OF TWO FROGS I Ring of children for pond. They supply the lines in italics.

16 CANDLES Probably best to let the story group say the whole poem while the lady and servants mime the action.

17 THE MICE AND THE CAT Children form a large ring and act as commentators. Four mice creep through a hole at one end. On the word HOME the cat wakes and chases them, trying to touch as many as possible before they leave the ring. The first one touched becomes Cat.

18 MISS MUFFET AND FRIEND Items 2 and 3 might be left until item 1 has been acted several times.

19 WE'RE ALL NODDING Repeat with 'skipping', dancing', etc. End by repeating 'nodding'.

20 MY PIGEON-HOUSE Group forms house by holding hands with pigeons inside. As they start to speak, they drop their hands and the pigeons fly out. The birds return during the second part and say the last two lines inside.

21 FOLLOW-MY-LEADER After practising this as a straight rhythm game, the leaders might assume different characters which the other children follow.

22 TADPOLES Group for pool; tadpoles, mother, water-rat.

24 OLD DAME Dame sits on a chair, and a line of children come towards her, holding hands. At the word 'chickens' she gets up and chases them. The first one caught becomes Dame.

25 THE TIRED CATERPILLAR The dots suggest a possible yawn before line 4.

26 THE SHEEP AND THE WOLF Shepherd on one side of acting-space, sheep on the other. Wolf hides round the corner. On the last line, sheep start crossing to shepherd; wolf comes from hiding and touches as many as he can.

26 THE LITTLE HUNTER Story group alters its way of saying the refrains to fit the changing moods.

27 WILLIE WILKIE Imagine a street with a double line of houses, each with a child inside. As Willie passes, tapping and listening at each house, the children jump into bed one after the other.

30 HOPPITY The teacher will certainly need to speak this one in order to keep the rhythm.

31 THE CANNY MOUSE Another for the teacher—at least in the early stages.

33 RAGGLE TAGGLE RABBIT-SKINS First stanza spoken by the story group (in the shape of a box or boxes); second stanza by the rabbits.

35 THE RABBIT AND THE FOX Story group may represent trees or hedge. Rabbit enters, hopping. Fox comes from behind

trees. An experiment might be made by adding an extra word to lines 1 and 3 in each stanza:

A rabbit came hopping, hopping, *hopping*

but this is more difficult because it gives the rabbit little time to rest.

36 HECTOR PROTECTOR Story group, Hector, the person who sends him (Lord Chamberlain?), king and queen.

37 THE WITCH AND THE WIZARD If the spells are spoken too loudly at first, it will be impossible to work up to a climax.

PART 2

42 CATCH-RHYMES Words and actions need to synchronise exactly, but the speakers should not be the movers. 4 The rowing rhythm of "Go, my little little boat" suggests a feather-stroke action.

46 TINKER, TAILOR Group says question lines. A different child answers each time, and mimes. Get children to add modern tradesmen.

47 WHEN I WAS A LADY Children add modern women: typist, teacher, mother, shop-girl, etc.

47 CROSSING THE STREAM Children need to visualise the situation as they 'cross' in single file, not too close together.

48 THE BUSY HOUSEWIVES One small group to speak lines 1, 2 and 3 in each verse; another for lines 4 and 5. A third group supplies the actions.

49 TELL ME HOW I'M WALKING To encourage clear mime and an exact use of words (softly, quickly, stealthily, etc.). When the class cannot guess the adverb, the teacher decides whether this is due to weak miming. Variety can be given by "Tell me how I'm *skipping*," etc.

50 SHEPHERD Dutch version of "The Sheep and the Wolf". (See p 26.)

52 JONATHAN BING Story group, Bing, soldier, archbishop and others. Bing speaks only the last four lines, while sitting at a table writing.

53 IN THE WOOD AT NIGHT One of those rhymes where the teacher may need to continue speaking the lines. The atmosphere and the quality of miming depend on this.

54 THE KING'S SPECTACLES James Gibson suggests sharing the first two verses between the king and two courtiers; the princess taking third verse; the hero appearing at the end of the fourth verse; and the king making the final proclamation. But the children may have other ideas.

55 KNIGHT AND LADY See general notes, p 115.

56 MAYPOLE DANCING A difficult one this: creating a maypole

dance without pole or ribbons! One group for words, one for actions.

57 THE FEET OF THE LAW The policeman walks while the villain lurks. Slow, steady speaking-pace until the words "terrible fright", when the policeman sees and chases the villain.

58 TRYING ON THE SLIPPER Begin with mime showing Ugly Sisters and Cinderella in kitchen, and arrival of Chamberlain and attendants. Then continue miming while a small group says the words; or else let Chamberlain and Ugly Sisters speak their own lines.

59 OLD WOMAN FROM THE WOOD Another formula for miming. The class guesses each woman's occupation.

60 THE CAT AND THE MOUSE Here the story group could say "Said she, said she", varying the tone to match each new development.

61 THE OLD WIVES Spoken by a small group and mimed in pairs.

62 THE PROUD TOWER Mary Cousins suggests: "The Tower is represented by a ring of children holding their hands high to keep out the soldiers. They speak the Tower's part in chorus. In the last verse they drop hands and turn facing the soldiers, who march in."

63 DANGER: WITCHES AT WORK! A little covey of witches round a cauldron. List of ingredients by separate witches until the words "front-door mat". After that they speak together, the final line being spoken by one very characterful witch.

64 THE MAGIC CLOAK This calls for quite accomplished miming by the boy and the townsfolk.

65 LABURNUM WALK The class divides into groups. Each group decides on a mime, and practises before showing it to the class.

66 THE THREE DUKES Mother and three daughters on one side of the acting-space; the dukes enter from the other side on imaginary horses.

67 THE RECRUITING SERGEANT Miming to accompany the story group. Later a complete acting scene might be developed, creating a crowd in an English market place in the eighteenth century, complete with dialogue.

68 KING ALFRED Even if acted on stage, the props should consist of nothing but a chair (perhaps on a rostrum) and this should be a plain one because it has to serve for a cottage seat as well as a throne. As with genuine ballads, the speaking should keep a sensible balance between sense-stress and metre. Nothing is more painful than to hear children chanting:

> . . . Laid aside his golden crown
> AND his sword of state.

The stress needs to fall quite naturally:

> And his swòrd of stàte.

74 CATCH-RHYMES Children can be asked for their ideas on what actions fit the words. 1 Fairly staccato speaking to encourage brisk marching. Marchers miss and 'change step' on lines 5 and 6. 2 Two or three workmen round a spike in the road. Strong hammer-beat on 'strong', 'heavy', 'bang' and 'clang'. 3 The scythe is a long farming implement once used for harvesting, not the short sickle. 4 Halliard chanty. One group says story-lines; one the refrains; a third group pulls on ropes. There are two strong beats in each line to accompany two vigorous downward pulls (left and right hand):

> A Yànkee ship came dòwn the river,
> Blòw, boys, blòw.

76 STATUES Each mimer invents his own actions. All stop on the word STILL and keep the position they happen to be in. They retain it through the second stanza until LIVE when the actions continue. Later, consider having other people besides dancers.

78 THE STREET-SELLERS Each rhyme is a genuine London street-cry of the seventeenth or eighteenth century. Opening and closing dialogue has been added, but the rest of the conversations are left to the children's invention. Each seller should have a clear idea of his character, his trade and his actions.

81 THE OLD STEAM-TRAIN Tricky lines to speak. They should be left to the teacher in the early stages.

82 OVERHEARD ON A SALTMARSH This is a poem rather than a rhyme. Great care is needed by both the speakers to catch and hold the atmosphere.

83 CLOWN Group speaks while the clown, with imaginary umbrella, walks an imaginary tightrope—a chalk line on the floor?

84 LONDON WALL Eleanor Farjeon wrote: "The Roman builds up London Wall with big and little bricks during the first verse. During the second verse he mounts on a stool behind the wall of children, looking down on them. During the third and fourth verses, children representing single features of London might range themselves in front of the wall, such as a church, a prison, a tree in a park, etc. The first verse the Roman says by himself; the rest of the verses can be distributed at will, but the bricks should always speak the refrain in the second line. In the sixth verse the wall begins to give way as London spreads through it. In the seventh verse the wall divides; the game ends with everyone falling flat, and the Roman spread-eagled on the ground in the middle of them."

86 THE BALLAD OF JOHN BLUNT A little-known English version of "Get up and bar the door."

88 KING JOHN Story group and seven knights. The king sits at a table with papers before him, reacts to each speaker in turn, and finally signs reluctantly.

89 BELL-RINGING Firm, steady speaking by one group while another group acts as ringers. The bell is a heavy one. The pull comes on the first word in every second and fourth line. During lines 1 and 3 the rope (with the ringer's hands) is drawn upwards. There is a slight 'hold' at the end of these lines as he prepares for the next downward effort.

90 THE THREE TINKERS Mother, three daughters and five separate groups of three suitors each: tinkers, tailors, soldiers, sailors and kings. Later discuss the following possibility: there are only three men in all—they return in different disguises.

92 GOING TO THE FAIR Each verse is acted by a different speaker: horse dealer, fruit seller, odd-job man, gypsy girl, travelling barber. After saying his two lines, he makes some spontaneous remarks 'in character'. (See example in square brackets.)

94 BAD SIR BRIAN BOTANY Story group, Sir Brian and villagers. Quite a lot of practice will be needed to get dovetailing of words and actions.

99 SINK SONG Group accompanies itself with appropriate scouring motions, suggesting unsavoury contents.

100 YOUNG EAGLE-FEATHER Based on "Hiawatha" rhythm, but should not become a jingle. The teacher says the lines until the natural speech-pattern is established. Later, two groups might share the lines. Aim at a build-up of excitement and tension. The deer, of course, is imaginary.

101 THE REVOLVING DOOR Give the words to two boys, without comment, and send them away to practise!

102 THE DRAGON Story group; knight; four to five children for dragon; others representing trees in forest.

104 FOUR CHARACTERS The children may be left to work these out for themselves. Characterisation and humour. Costumes and props permitted.

106 KING CANUTE A platform or series of rostra at the back of the acting-space will give the impression of a pier and esplanade, and will also assist the grouping.

ACKNOWLEDGEMENTS

Grateful acknowledgement is made to the following authors, agents and publishers for permission to include copyright material:

Evelyn Abraham for "Bunny Rabbit, bunny rabbit" and "One, two, three".

Hilda Adams for "Fiddle me up to London Town", "Here we come galloping", "Left, right; left, right" and "Farmer Brown".

Basil Blackwell & Mott Ltd for "Here Comes a Knight", "The Hare" and "Shepherd" by Rose Fyleman from *Widdy-Widdy-Wurkey*.

Mollie Clarke for "Raggle Taggle Rabbit-Skins".

Mary Cousins for "The Proud Tower" from *Invitation to the Play Part 1* (Nelson, London).

J.B. Cramer & Co Ltd for "The King of Candy" by Anne Harding Thompson.

Duckworth & Co Ltd for Harold Monro's "Overheard on a Saltmarsh" from his *Collected Poems*.

Evans Brothers Limited for H.S. Bennett's "Follow-My-Leader" from *My First Jingle Book* and Ruth Ainsworth's "Candles" from *Child Education*.

William Heinemann Ltd for "Mr Tom Narrow" by James Reeves from *The Wandering Moon*.

David Higham Associates for "Harold" by Eleanor Farjeon from *Tunes for a Penny Piper*, Eleanor Farjeon for "London Wall" from *Nursery Rhymes of London Town* (Duckworth).

J.A. Lindon for "Sink Song".

Methuen & Co Ltd for "King John" by Hugh Chesterman from *Kings and Other Things*.

C.R. Milne and Methuen Childrens Books Ltd for "Hoppity" from *Now We Are Six* and "Bad Sir Brian Botany" from *When We Were Very Young*, both by A.A. Milne.

Pitman Publishing for "The Old Green Gnome" by Maisie Cobby from *We Play and Grow* and "What are you going to be?" by Paul Edmonds from *Rhymes for Children*.

Ian Serraillier and Oxford University Press for his poem "Too Polite" from *Happily Ever After*.

The Society of Authors as the literary representative of the Estate of Rose Fyleman for "Tadpoles" and "The Little Hunter".

World's Work Ltd for "Jonathan Bing Visits the King" by Beatrice Curtis Brown from *Jonathan Bing*.

We should also like to acknowledge those editors who first collected the following anonymous rhymes:

W.S. & C. Baring-Gould for the first item under "Rhymes about Robin", recorded in their Annotated Mother Goose (Bramhall House Publishing Co, New York).

William Cole for the second item under "Miss Muffet and Friends" and "The Wicked Burglar" from *Rhyme Giggles: Nonsense Giggles* (Bodley Head).

Iona and Peter Opie for "Little Miss Tuckett" and "The Recruiting Sergeant" ·which appear in their *Puffin Book of Nursery Rhymes* (Penguin).

Nicholas Tucker for "The Pirate Chief" and "The Railway Navvy" from his *Mother Goose Lost* (Hamish Hamilton Ltd).

It has not been possible in every case to trace the authors of poems. If any acknowledgement has been omitted, the publishers offer their apologies and will rectify this in future printings on notification being received.

INDEX OF TITLES

INDEX OF FIRST LINES